KETO DIET COOKBOOK FOR BEGINNERS

The Bible of ketogenic cooking. 1500 days of tasty and easy-to-cook recipes. Discover how to make delicious this healthy lifestyle. FULL COLOR EDITION

D1716294

Margaret Salt

Table of content

INTRODUCTION 6

CHAPTER 1. GETTING INTO KETOSIS 8

1.1. KETO-FLU, AND HOW DOES IT AFFECT YOU? 8
1.2. GETTING RID OF THE KETO FLU 8
1.3. FOODS TO STAY AWAY FROM 9
1.4. FOODS TO EAT.. 9

CHAPTER 2. BENEFITS OF KETO DIET 11

KETOGENIC RECIPES 14

GREEN EGGS..15
SIMPLE BREAKFAST SANDWICH 16
CREAM CHEESE PANCAKE 17
MUSHROOM EGG BAKES 18
KETO MUG BREAD 19
CHICKEN SALAD WITH CHIMICHURRI DRESSING 20
ASIAN CHICKEN STIR-FRY..21
GREEK CHICKEN 22
CREAM CHEESE, BACON, CHEDDAR CHICKEN 24
EASY LETTUCE WRAP 25
KETO BUTTER BURGERS 26
KETO PIZZA 28
STUFFED SAUSAGES.. 29
BACON WRAPPED OVEN CHICKEN SKEWERS 30
BAKED CHICKEN & VEGGIES 31
KETO TUNA SALAD 32
KETO SHRIMP & GRITS 33
AHI POKE BOWL 34
TUNA ZUCCHINI BOATS 35
BAKED SALMON 36
COCONUT MILK POPSICLES 38
WHITE CHOCOLATE AND PEANUT BUTTER FAT BOMBS........................39
CHOCOLATE MUG CAKE 40
CHOCO-ORANGE BALLS..41
CHOCO-COFFEE CANDY.. 42
KETO PEANUT BUTTER 43
KETO SNACK BARS 44
ROSEMARY SPICED NUTS 45
SEED BREAD LOAF.. 46
BROCCOLI TOTS 47
ZUCCHINI NOODLES 48
VEGETABLE SOUP... 49
CAULIFLOWER MAC & CHEESE 50
BLUEBERRY PLEASURE SMOOTHIE 51
CHEESE & SPINACH PIE 52
BROCCOLI SALAD... 53
DEVILED EGGS (MAYO-LESS) 54
EGG SALAD 55
CAULIFLOWER "BREADSTICKS" 56
LOADED CAULIFLOWER 57
CREAMY CHICKEN GARLIC SOUP...58

CREAM OF CAULIFLOWER *59*
CREAMY ASPARAGUS SOUP *60*
KETO CHEESEBURGER SOUP...*61*
CREAM OF MUSHROOMS SOUP *62*
BERRIES & CREAM SHAKE *63*
STRAWBERRY CHIA ZUCCHINI SMOOTHIE *64*
PEANUT BUTTER SMOOTHIE.. *65*
AVOCADO MINT SMOOTHIE... *66*
DOUBLE CHOCOLATE SMOOTHIE *67*

4 WEEK MEAL PLAN **68**

CONCLUSION **70**

Introduction

The keto diet is a low-carb, high-fat diet that resembles the Atkins diet in many ways. It requires substantially lowering carbohydrate consumption and substituting fat. This decrease in carbohydrates causes you to initiate a metabolic state called ketosis.

Your organs become very effective at consuming fat for energy when this occurs. It also causes fat to be converted to ketones inside the liver, which may be used to provide fuel to the brain.

Ketogenic diets may lower insulin and blood sugar levels considerably. This, along with the increasing number of ketones, offers a number of health advantages.

When you consume fewer than 50 grams of carbohydrates each day, your body soon runs out of blood sugar. This usually takes three to four days. Then you'll begin to break down fat and protein for energy, perhaps resulting in weight loss. Ketosis is the term for this state. It's vital to remember that the ketogenic lifestyle is short-term designed to help you lose weight rather than improve your health.

A ketogenic diet is most often used to reduce weight, but it may also be used to treat medical disorders such as epilepsy. It may also assist those with heart disease, some brain illnesses, and even pimples, but more study is needed in those areas. Consult your doctor first to see whether a ketogenic diet is right for you, particularly if you do have type 1 diabetes.

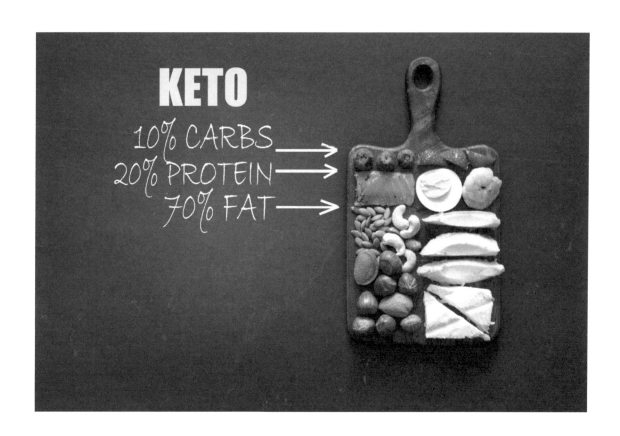

Chapter 1. Getting into Ketosis

The basic purpose of the keto diet is to maintain you in ketosis at all times. You should take up to 25 g of carbohydrates per day if you're just starting out on the keto diet.

You get keto-adapted/ fat-adapted after being in ketosis for a lengthy period of time (approximately 4 to 8 weeks). When your glycogen (the glucose glycogen in the muscles and liver) levels drop, you lose water weight, your muscular endurance improves, and your total energy levels rise.

Another advantage of becoming keto-adapted is that you would sustain ketosis by eating less than 50 g of net carbohydrates per day.

1.1. Keto-Flu, and how does it affect you?

The keto flu is a flu-like condition that often occurs among keto dieters owing to low electrolyte levels.

Symptoms may include:

- Fatigue
- Nausea
- Cough
- Sniffles
- Headaches
- Irritability

It's crucial to remember that this isn't the flu! Because of the same symptoms, it's dubbed keto flu, although it's not infectious and doesn't include a virus.

What Causes It to Happen?

The major cause of keto flu is a deficiency in electrolytes, particularly sodium. When you first start keto, you eliminate a lot of manufactured meals and replace them with more full, natural foods. Although this is excellent, it results in a sharp decrease in salt consumption.

Furthermore, cutting carbohydrates lowers insulin levels, which lowers salt deposited in the kidneys. You end up deficient in sodium and other electrolytes as a result of your lower salt intake. Getting adequate electrolytes, particularly sodium, might help you prevent the keto flu.

1.2. Getting Rid of the Keto Flu

Adding additional salt and electrolytes to the diet is the greatest approach to prevent (or cure) the keto flu. Here are some of the most effective (and delicious) methods to increase salt intake:

- Increasing the amount of salt in your meals
- Soup broth to drink
- Consuming salty foods such as bacon and pickled veggies

To avoid getting the keto flu, consume extra salt when you first start the keto diet. If you do get it, keep in mind that it will pass soon, and you will emerge as a fat-burning machine!

1.3. Foods to stay away from

Grains and Starches

Remove all cereals, kinds of pasta, and loaves of bread, rice, potatoes, maize, oats, quinoa, flour, bagels, croissants, and wraps from your diet.

Everything Sweet

Refined sugar, sweets, fountain drinks, fruit juices, pastries, candy bars, milk chocolate, and so on should all be avoided.

Legumes

Any peas, beans, or lentils should be thrown out or donated.

Oils from vegetables and seeds

Stop using sunflower, soybean, canola, maize, safflower, and grapeseed oil, as well as other vegetable and seed oils. Remove trans fats from your diet, such as margarine.

Examine the Nutritional Labels

Check all of your items' nutrition labels to determine whether they're rich in carbohydrates. Avoid items with a long list of unintelligible components. Less is typically preferable to more. Always double-check the carb counts versus the serving sizes. Manufacturers might occasionally prescribe incomprehensibly tiny serving sizes to ostensibly lower calorie and carbohydrate counts.

Something may seem to be low in carbohydrates at first appearance, but a simple comparison to serving size reveals that the product is primarily sugar. Maintain vigilance!

Now that you've gotten rid of just about everything you do not need, it's time to replenish your pantry and refrigerator with tasty and nutritious keto-friendly items that will help with weight loss, get healthier, and feel great!

1.4. Foods to eat

With these in your house, you will always be ready for keto.

Meat, Eggs and Fish

Almost all meats, eggs and fish are perfect for keto.

Vegetables

Eat non-starchy vegetables like asparagus, mushrooms, cucumber, lettuce, broccoli, onions, peppers, Brussels sprouts, tomatoes, garlic, cauliflower, and zucchini.

Dairy

You may use full-fat dairies such as sour cream, butter, cheeses, heavy (whipping) cream, and unsweetened yogurt.

Although they are not dairy, unsweetened coconut milk and almond milk are good milk substitutes.

Avoid skim milk, regular milk, and sugar yogurts because of sugar. Don't use all low-fat and fat-free dairy products.

Oils and Fats

Olive oil, butter, avocado oil, and bacon fat are good for cooking.

Fruits

Berries like blueberries, raspberries, strawberries, etc., are allowed in little amounts. Avocados are great!

Sweeteners

Stevia and erythritol.

Miscellaneous

A lot of water, unsweetened tea, and coffee

Condiments like mustard, pesto, mayonnaise and sriracha

Broths

Pickles and fermented foods

Nuts and seeds (chia seeds, pecans, almonds, flaxseeds, macadamias, walnuts, etc.)

Chapter 2. Benefits of Keto Diet

The ketogenic diet has many benefits, including and not limited to:

1. Aids in weight reduction

The ketogenic diet may assist in weight loss. The keto may help you lose weight in a variety of ways, including by increasing your metabolism and decreasing your hunger

Ketogenic diets consist of meals that fill you up and may help you lose weight by lowering hunger-stimulating hormones.

In a meta-analysis published in 2013, a review of 11 research found that participants who followed a keto lost 5 pounds more after 6 months than those who followed a low-fat diet.

2. Helps with acne

Acne may be caused by a variety of factors, including nutrition and blood sugar levels in certain individuals. Eating a diet heavy in highly processed carbs may imbalance gut bacteria equilibrium and drive blood sugar to dramatically fluctuate, both of which would be harmful to skin health.

3. Has the potential to lessen the risk of some cancers.

The ketogenic diet has been studied to see whether it may help prevent or perhaps cure some malignancies. According to Trusted Source, keto could be a safe and effective supplemental treatment for persons who are undergoing chemotherapy or radiation therapy for certain malignancies. It is because it would induce cancer cells to experience more oxidative stress than normal cells, leading them to perish.

More recent research was conducted. According to a 2018 Trusted Source, since the keto diet decreases sugar in the blood, it can also reduce the insulin issue risks. Insulin is a blood sugar-controlling hormone that has been linked to several cancers.

Although research in this area is limited, according to Trusted Source, keto could have some benefits in cancer therapy. To completely comprehend the potential advantages of keto in cancer treatment, additional research is needed.

4. It has the potential to enhance heart health.

When following the keto, it is critical to consume nutritious meals. According to some studies, eating good fats such as avocados in place of bad fats like rinds may assist improve cardiovascular health by lowering cholesterol.

Cholesterol levels that are too high may raise the risk of heart disease. As a result of the keto diet's cholesterol-lowering effects, a person's risk of cardiac problems may be reduced.

The analysis found, however, that the good benefits of nutrition on heart health are conditional on diet quality. As a result, it's critical to consume nutritious, well-balanced foods when on the keto diet.

5. It has the potential to protect brain function.

According to certain research, ketones produced during the keto diet have neuroprotective properties, meaning they help strengthen and protect brain and nerve cells. As a result, a keto diet may aid in the prevention or management of illnesses such as Alzheimer's disease. However, additional study into the effects of a keto diet on the brain is required.

6. Has the potential to lessen seizure frequency.

A keto diet's fat, protein, and carbohydrate ratio changes how the body utilizes energy. Ketosis is a metabolic condition during which your body consumes ketone bodies as an energy source.

Ketosis, according to the Epilepsy Foundation, may help patients with epilepsy, particularly those who haven't responded to previous treatments. More study is needed to establish how helpful this is, although it seems to help children with focal seizures the most. The concept that a ketogenic diet may help persons with epilepsy is supported by Trusted Source. The keto diet may help with epilepsy symptoms in a variety of ways.

7. Helps with PCOS symptoms

Excess male hormones, polycystic ovaries and ovulatory dysfunction are all symptoms of polycystic ovarian syndrome (PCOS), a hormonal condition. Skin issues and weight gain are common side effects of a high-carbohydrate diet in patients with PCOS.

The keto and PCOS are the subjects of a few clinical investigations. Over the course of 24 weeks, five women were studied in a 2005 pilot study by Trusted Source. A ketogenic diet improved multiple indicators of PCOS.

According to a separate assessment of data by 2019Trusted Source, a keto diet may help persons with hormonal diseases like PCOS and type 2 diabetes. They did warn, however, that the results were too mixed to endorse a ketogenic diet as a therapy for PCOS as a whole..

KETOGENIC RECIPES

GREEN EGGS

INGREDIENTS

- 1½ TBSP. OF RAPESEED OIL
- 2 CLOVES OF SLICED GARLIC
- 2 LEEKS, TRIMMED AND SLICED
- ½ TSP. OF CORIANDER SEEDS
- A PINCH OF CHILI FLAKES
- ½ TSP. OF FENNEL SEEDS
- SPINACH
- 2 TBSP. OF GREEK YOGURT
- 2 EGGS, LARGE
- 1 LEMON, SQUEEZED

15 MINUTES   2 SERVINGS

Instructions:

- In a pan, heat the oil. Cook until the leek is tender, adding a touch of salt.

- Combine the garlic, coriander, fennel, and chili flakes in a mixing bowl. Once the seeds have started to crackle, add the spinach, and reduce the heat. Stir until the spinach has withered and decreased, then push it to one side of the grill.

- Pour a little amount of oil into the saucepan, then break in the eggs and cook until they are done to your preference.

- Season with salt and pepper after mixing the yogurt into the spinach mixture. To serve, pile the salad onto plates, top with the fried egg, drizzle a little lemon over the top, and sprinkle with pepper and chili flakes.

Nutritional Values: **Calories** *298 kcal | Protein 18g | Fat 20g| Carbs 8g | Salt 0.8g |Sugar 6g |Fibers 6g*

SIMPLE BREAKFAST SANDWICH

INGREDIENTS

- 2 EGGS
- 2 TBSP. OF CREAM CHEESE
- 4 SAUSAGE PATTIES
- 4 TBSP. OF SHARP CHEDDAR
- ½ TSP. SRIRACHA
- ½ AVOCADO, MEDIUM, SLICED
- SALT AND PEPPER

5 MINUTES   2 SERVINGS

Instructions:

- Cook sausages according to package directions in a pan over medium heat and put them aside.

- Combine cream cheese with sharp cheddar in a small mixing bowl. Microwave on high for 20-30 secs, or until completely melted.

- Mix with sriracha and set aside

- Make a tiny omelet using the egg and seasonings.

- Assemble the sandwich by filling the omelet with the cheese sriracha mix.

Nutritional Values: Calories 603 kcal | Protein 22g | Fat 54g | Carbs 7g | Salt 235mg | Sugar 6g | Fibers 3g

CREAM CHEESE PANCAKE

INGREDIENTS

- 4 OZ. CREAM CHEESE
- 2 EGGS, LARGE
- ¼ CUP ALMOND FLOUR
- ½ TSP. BAKING POWDER
- COOKING SPRAY
- ¼ TSP. OF FINE SALT
- SLICED STRAWBERRIES

5 MINUTES 2 SERVINGS

Instructions:

- In a blender, combine the cream cheese, flour, baking powder, eggs, and salt until smooth.

- Over medium heat, heat a large Teflon frying pan. Cooking spray or butter should be used to coat the pan. Add 2 to 2 1/2 tbsp of the batter into the melted butter. Wait until the bottom is a rich golden-brown color, approximately 3 minutes. Cook for another 1 to 2 minutes, or until the reverse section is golden brown. Place on a platter to cool.

- Cook the remaining batter in the same manner. Serve with powdered sugar and sliced strawberries, or sprinkle with maple syrup. Makes roughly 6 little pancakes, each about 4 inches wide, for 2 people

Nutritional Values: Calories 329 kcal | Protein 10.1 g | Fat 30.2 g | Carbs 5.4 g | Salt 0.5g |Sugar 2.9 g |Fibers 1.3 g

MUSHROOM EGG BAKES

INGREDIENTS

- 1 TBSP. OLIVE OIL, EXTRA-VIRGIN
- 1/4 CUP OF SHALLOTS, MINCED
- COOKING SPRAY
- 1/4 CUP OF MOZZARELLA CHEESE, SHREDDED
- 4 OZ. MIXED MUSHROOMS OF CHOICE, FRESH, SLICED
- 3 EGGS, LARGE
- 1 TBSP. OF FRESH THYME, CHOPPED
- 1/4 CUP OF WHOLE MILK
- 1/4 TSP. OF BLACK PEPPER, GROUND
- 1/4 TSP. OF KOSHER SALT

10 MINUTES   2 SERVINGS

Instructions:

- Preheat the oven to 400°F and place a rack in the center. Using a little butter or cooking spray, coat 4 ramekins. Set aside the ramekins on such a rimmed baking sheet to make moving them to and from the oven simpler.

- In a small saucepan, heat the olive oil over moderate heat until it shimmers. Take the shallot and cook for 3 minutes, or until tender and transparent. Cook, occasionally stirring, until the mushrooms are softened and aromatic, approximately 5 minutes. Remove the pan from the heat and stir in thyme.

- In a medium mixing bowl, whisk together the eggs, salt, milk, and pepper. Evenly distribute the mushroom mixture among the ramekins. Distribute the cheese evenly among the mushrooms. Put the egg sauce on top, ending just below the ramekin's top.

- Set the baking sheet inside the oven to bake for 20 to 25 minutes, or until the tops are brown and puff somewhat and the eggs are totally set.

- Enjoy while it's still warm!

Nutritional Values: Calories 287 kcal | Protein 16.2 g | Fat 21.5 g | Carbs 8.3 g | Salt 0.7g |Sugar 4.9 g |Fibers 1.

KETO MUG BREAD

INGREDIENTS

- 1 TSP. OF BAKING POWDER
- 6 TBSP. OF ALMOND FLOUR
- 2 EGGS
- ½ TSP. OF SALT
- 2 PINCHES OF BLACK PEPPER, GROUND
- 4 TBSP. OF BUTTER, MELTED
- 2 PINCHES OF GARLIC POWDER

1 MINUTES   2 SERVINGS

Instructions:

- In a small mixing dish, combine all of the items except 1 tbsp melted butter.

- Whisk everything together well.

- Spoon the mixture into a microwave-safe mug that has been gently buttered.

- Microwave on high for 90 seconds.

- Remove the cup from the microwave and pour the leftover melted butter over it. Take the bread from the cup, slice it, and then spread the remaining butter on top.

- Enjoy while it's still warm

Nutritional Values: *Calories 390 kcal | Protein 10g | Fat 37g | Carbs 3g | Salt 60 mg |Sugar 60 mg |Fibers 50 mg*

CHICKEN SALAD WITH CHIMICHURRI DRESSING

INGREDIENTS

- 4 TBSP. OF MAYONNAISE
- CHIMICHURRI DRESSING
- 1/4 TBSP. OF RED WINE VINEGAR
- 1/2 TBSP. OF CHOPPED RED CHILI PEPPERS
- 1/2 CUP OF FRESH PARSLEY
- 1 CLOVE OF GARLIC
- 1 TBSP. OF OREGANO, DRIED

CHICKEN THIGHS
- 1 LB. OF CHICKEN THIGHS, BONELESS
- 1 TBSP. OF OLIVE OIL
- SALT AND PEPPER

SERVING
- 1 SLICED AVOCADO
- 2 CUPS LEAFY GREENS
- 1/4 SLICED RED ONION
- 1/2 SLICED RED CHILI PEPPER
- 1 WEDGED LEMON

15 MINUTES   2 SERVINGS

Instructions:

- In a blender, combine all of the contents for the chimichurri dressing. Blend until completely smooth. If you want a runnier consistency, add additional water.
- Using olive oil, heat a big skillet. Using salt and pepper, rub the chicken thighs. Put them in the heated pan and cook them along both sides until done. It will take roughly 15-20 minutes.
- Prepare the veggies and serve them on plates or a large serving tray while the meat is cooking. Place the chicken on top along with lemon wedges, the dressing, and chili if you want the meal to be a little spicier.

Nutritional Values: Calories 713kcal | Protein 49g | Fat 52g | Carbs 15g | Salt 25 mg |Sugar 10 mg |Fibers 10g

ASIAN CHICKEN STIR-FRY

INGREDIENTS

SPICY MAYONNAISE
- 1/4 CUP OF MAYONNAISE
- 1/2 TSP. OF GARLIC POWDER
- 1 TBSP. OF HOT SAUCE

CHICKEN STIR FRY WITH BROCCOLI
- 1 TBSP. OF OLIVE OIL
- 1 LB. OF THIN-SLICED BONELESS CHICKEN THIGHS
- 1/2 TSP. OF BLACK PEPPER, GROUNDED
- 1 1/2 CUPS OF BROCCOLI, CHOPPED
- 1/2 TSP. OF GARLIC POWDER
- 1 TBSP. OF TAMARI SOY SAUCE

15 MINUTES   2 SERVINGS

Instructions:

Spicy mayonnaise

- In a small mixing dish, add the components and whisk to incorporate.

- Broccoli and chicken stir-fry

- In a wok or big frying pan, heat the oil over moderate flame. Combine the garlic powder, chicken, and pepper in a mixing bowl. Stir-fry the chicken for a few minutes until golden brown.

- Combine the broccoli with tamari soy sauce in the pan. Stir everything together for a few minutes, till the broccoli is crispy but still tender. Serve with spicy mayonnaise.

Nutritional Values: Calories 613kcal | Protein 43g | Fat 46g | Carbs 7g | Salt 85 mg |Sugar 25 mg |Fibers 2g

GREEK CHICKEN

INGREDIENTS

- 3/4 TSP. OF SEA SALT
- 1/2 LB. OF CHICKEN BREAST
- 1 1/2 TBSP. OF OLIVE OIL
- 1/4 TSP. OF BLACK PEPPER
- 1/2 TBSP. OF BALSAMIC VINEGAR)
- 5 OZ. OF ZUCCHINI, SLICED
- 1/4 LARGE ONION, CUT TO HALF-MOONS
- 1/4 LB. GRAPE TOMATOES HALVED
- 1/4 TBSP. OF DRIED PARSLEY
- 1/4 TBSP. OF DRIED DILL
- 1/2 TSP. OF GARLIC POWDER
- 1/ TSP. OF DRIED OREGANO
- 1/5 CUP OF FETA CHEESE, CRUMBLED, OPTIONAL

20 MINUTES   2 SERVINGS

Instructions:

- Heat the oven to 400F. Foil an extra big sheet pan and oil it generously.

- Fill a large mixing bowl halfway with water. Stir in 2 teaspoons sea salt to dissolve. Add chicken and set it aside to marinate for 20 minutes.

- Meantime, prep the vegetables: grape tomatoes, zucchini, and onions.

- Combine the parsley, oregano, dried dill, and garlic powder in a small dish.

- Once the chicken has finished marinating, pat it dry and arrange it in a single layer on the baking tray, close but not touched.

- Rub the chicken from both sides with 1 tablespoon oil. Sprinkle both sides of the chickens with 3/4 teaspoon sea salt and 1/4 teaspoon black pepper. Half of the herb combination should be used on both sides.

- Meanwhile, combine the chopped veggies with the leftover 2 tablespoons oil in a large mixing dish. Combine the remaining 3/4 teaspoon sea salt, 1/4 teaspoon black pepper, and the remainder of the herb combination in a mixing bowl. Toss well to combine. Arrange the vegetables on the baking tray in a single layer, ensuring sure they don't cover the chicken.

- Drizzle the balsamic vinegar well over chicken and vegetables. (Alternatively, you may mix some with the vegetables and sprinkle the remainder over the chicken.)
- Bake the chicken and vegetables for approximately 20 minutes, or until the vegetables are tender and the chicken is fully cooked. Remove the baking dish and set it aside to cool for 5 minutes.
- Transfer the chicken to dinner prep containers after slicing it. Fill the remaining space with vegetables.

Nutritional Values: *Calories 287 kcal | Protein 7g | Fat 15g | Carbs 7g | Salt 90 mg |Sugar 4g |Fibers 1g*

CREAM CHEESE, BACON, CHEDDAR CHICKEN

INGREDIENTS

- 2 CHICKEN BREASTS, SLICED IN HALF
- 1/2 TBSP. OF OLIVE OIL
- SALT AND PEPPER
- 4 STRIPS OF COOKED BACON, CHOPPED
- 3 OZ. OF CREAM CHEESE, COLD, SLICED INTO 8
- 1/2 CUP OF SHREDDED CHEDDAR CHEESE

30 MINUTES   2 SERVINGS

Instructions:

- Preheat oven to 375 degrees Fahrenheit.

- Olive oil should be used to coat the base of the casserole dish.

- In a casserole dish, place the chicken breasts. Split in half horizontally to form 4 thin chicken breasts.

- Season both sides of the chicken breasts using pepper and salt. Cream cheese should be spread on top.

- Put chopped fried bacon on top. Shredded Cheddar cheese is sprinkled on top.

- Cook for 20-30 minutes, uncovered, till chicken fully cooked through. The amount of time it takes to cook your chicken breasts is determined by their thickness.

Nutritional Values: Calories 602 kcal | Protein 39g | Fat 47g | Carbs 2g | Salt 734 mg |Sugar 1g |Fibers 90 mg

EASY LETTUCE WRAP

INGREDIENTS

- 1/4 CUP OF CHOPPED ONION
- 1 CHICKEN BREAST
- SALT AND PEPPER
- 1 CHOPPED GREEN ONION
- 2 LARGE LETTUCE LEAVES
- 1/5 CUP OF CANNED WATER CHESTNUTS, CHOPPED

HOMEMADE HOISIN SAUCE
- 2/3 TBSP. OF PEANUT BUTTER, NATURAL
- 1 2/3 TBSP. LOW SODIUM SOY SAUCE
- 2/3 CLOVES OF MINCED GARLIC CLOVES
- 2/3 TSP. OF SESAME OIL
- 1/3 TSP. OF HOT SAUCE
- 2/3 TSP. OF UNSWEETENED AND UNSEASONED RICE WINE VINEGAR
- 0.17 TEASPOON GARLIC POWDER
- 1/3 TBSP. OF ZERO-CALORIE SWEETENER
- SALT AND PEPPER

10 MINUTES 2 SERVINGS

Instructions:

Hoisin Sauce (Homemade)

- In a small mixing dish, mix all of the ingredients. Mix thoroughly.

Filling for Lettuce Wraps

- Using moderate heat, heat a pan. In the same pan, add the ground chicken. Season using pepper and salt.

- Crumble the ground chicken using a spatula or a big spoon. Cook for 3 to 4 minutes, just until the chicken is golden brown. Excess fat should be drained if necessary.

- Add the onions to the mix. Cook, occasionally stirring, for 2 minutes, just until the onions are aromatic.

- Combine the homemade hoisin sauce, water chestnuts, and green onions in the same pan. Add another 1-2 minutes to the cooking time.

- Fill the lettuce with the filling. Green onions go on top. Serve!

Nutritional Values Calories 197kcal | Protein 16g | Fat 12g | Carbs 4g | Salt 800mg |Sugar 1g |Fibers 2g

KETO BUTTER BURGERS

INGREDIENTS

- 1/2 TSP. OF SALT
- 1/2 LB. OF 80/20 GROUND BEEF
- 1/4 TSP. OF BLACK PEPPER, GROUND
- 1/2 FRESHLY CUT JALAPEÑO
- 1/4 OF CHOPPED RED ONION
- 1/2 THINLY SLICED TOMATO
- 1/2 AVOCADO, CUT LENGTHWISE
- 1/2 BUTTERHEAD LETTUCE
- 4 SLICES OF CHEDDAR CHEESE
- 1/2 OZ. OF SLICED BUTTER

10 MINUTES   2 SERVINGS

Instructions:

- Preheat the grill on medium heat for 20 minutes. These delectable burgers may also be made on the stovetop. Simply cook the patties in butter for several minutes on each side in a frying pan.

- Combine the salt, ground beef, and pepper in a mixing bowl.

- The onion should be finely chopped, and the jalapeno should be sliced into tiny pieces. If you don't want it to be overly hot, remove the seeds beforehand. Mix the onion & jalapeno into the meat with your hands until everything is well combined.

- Make one hamburger patty for each serving. Form them into a sphere first, then gently push down. If you're grilling them, leave them a little thicker since they cook quickly.

- According to how cooked you want your patties, grill them on each side. Allow for a 10-minute break before serving to allow the juices to settle.

- Slice the tomato thinly while the patties are on the pan. Cut the avocado in half lengthwise, scoop out the flesh, and discard the pit.

- Use 3-4 salad leaves for every burger. Place a patty in the center and top with cheese slices and a piece of butter. Sprinkle with salt and insert the tomato and avocado. Wrap the burger with plastic wrap to make it easier to grasp.

Nutritional Values: *Calories 530kcal | Protein 31g | Fat 42g | Carbs 4g | Salt 1g |Sugar 2g |Fibers 4g*

KETO PIZZA

INGREDIENTS

- CRUST
- 1 ½ CUPS MOZZARELLA CHEESE, SHREDDED
- 4 EGGS

TOPPING
- 1 TSP. OF DRIED OREGANO
- 3 TBSP. OF TOMATO SAUCE, UNSWEETENED
- 1 ½ OZ. OF PEPPERONI
- 1 ¼ CUPS OF PROVOLONE CHEESE, SHREDDED
- OLIVES

FOR SERVING
- 1 CUP OF LEAFY GREENS
- ¼ CUP OF OLIVE OIL
- SALT AND PEPPER

25 MINUTES   2 SERVINGS

Instructions:

- Preheat oven to 375 degrees Fahrenheit.

- Begin by preparing the crust. In a medium-sized mixing dish, crack the eggs and add the shredded cheese. To combine, give it a thorough stir.

- Distribute the cheese and egg mixture on a baking sheet pan using a spatula. You have the option of making two circles or one huge rectangle pizza. Bake for 15 minutes, or until the pizza dough is golden brown. Remove from the oven and set aside to cool.

- Increase temperature to 450F. Apply tomato sauce to the crust and top with oregano. Arrange the pepperoni, then olives over the cheese

- Heat for a further 5-10 minutes, just until the pizza is golden brown.

- Serve with a side of fresh salad.

Nutritional Values: Calories 1024kcal | Protein 56g | Fat 86g | Carbs 8g | Salt 2g |Sugar 4g |Fibers 1g

STUFFED SAUSAGES

INGREDIENTS

- 2 STICKS OF MOZZARELLA CHEESE
- 2 LB. OF ITALIAN SAUSAGE LINKS
- 1/5 CUP MARINARA SAUCE

30 MINUTES   2 SERVINGS

Instruction:

- Preheat the oven to 400 degrees Fahrenheit.

- Cut a sausage along the side using kitchen scissors. Remove the casing only if absolutely necessary. Insert a mozzarella stick into the sausage and push it back into place. Place it in a baking pan, casing side down.

- Over the sausage, add the marinara sauce.

- Cook for 30-40 mins, or until a meat thermometer reads 160 degrees Fahrenheit.

Nutritional Values: Calories 431kcal | Protein 23g | Fat 36g | Carbs 2g | Salt 1072mg | Sugar 1g | Fibers 0g

BACON WRAPPED OVEN CHICKEN SKEWERS

INGREDIENTS

- 1/5 TBSP. OF OLIVE OIL
- 1/2 LB. OF SKINLESS, BONELESS CHICKEN BREASTS, CUT INTO 1-INCH CHUNKS
- 1/10 TSP. OF ONION POWDER
- 1/10 TSP. OF DRIED BASIL
- A PINCH OF CAYENNE PEPPER
- 1/10 TSP. OF SMOKED PAPRIKA
- SALT AND PEPPER
- 1/10 TSP. OF DRIED THYME
- 4 SLICES OF BACON, HALVED
- 1/10 TSP. OF GARLIC POWDER
- 2 GRILLING SKEWERS

25 MINUTES   2 SERVINGS

Instructions:

- Preheat the oven to 350 degrees Fahrenheit. Aluminum foil should be used to line a baking pan. Spray a wire rack with cooking oil and place on top of the baking sheet; set aside.

- Place the chicken in a large mixing basin and cut it into 1-inch chunks. Drizzle in the olive oil and whisk

- Sprinkle with salt, dried thyme, paprika, cayenne pepper, pepper, garlic powder, onion powder, and dried basil; toss thoroughly.

- Wrap a bacon piece around each chicken portion, and thread 6 or 5 pieces onto every skewer. So that the bacon pieces remain intact, put them closely together on the skewers.

- Place skewers atop the baking rack that has already been prepared. Bake for 30 minutes, or until the chicken is well cooked, and the bacon is crisp.

- Turn off the heat and set it aside to cool for 5 minutes. Serve.

Nutritional Values: Calories 117 kcal | Protein 19g | Fat 3g | Carbs 0g | Salt 105mg |Sugar 0g |Fibers 3g

BAKED CHICKEN & VEGGIES

INGREDIENTS

- COOKING SPRAY
- 1/2 TBSP. OF SESAME OIL
- 1/2 LB. OF BONELESS, SKINLESS CHICKEN BREASTS
- 1 TBSP. OF SOY SAUCE
- 1 DICED RED BELL PEPPERS
- 1 TBSP. OF HONEY
- 1 YELLOW DICED BELL PEPPERS
- 1/4 HEAD FLORIATED BROCCOLI
- 1 SLICED CARROTS
- 1 DICED RED ONIONS
- SALT AND PEPPER
- 1 TBSP. OF EXTRA-VIRGIN OLIVE OIL
- ¼ CUP OF FRESH PARSLEY, CHOPPED

25 MINUTES   2 SERVINGS

Instructions:

- Heat the oven to 400 degrees Fahrenheit. Using a nonstick spray, lightly coat a baking sheet.

- Arrange the chicken on the prepared baking sheet. Mix together the sesame oil with soy sauce in a mixing bowl. Coat the chicken with the mixture in an equal layer.

- On a baking sheet, place the yellow and red bell peppers, broccoli, carrots, and red onion. Sprinkle with salt after drizzling the oil over the veggies and gently tossing to cover.

- Roast for 20 to 25 minutes, or until the veggies are soft and the poultry is thoroughly cooked. Before serving, garnish with parsley.

Nutritional Values: Calories 380 kcal | Protein 31g | Fat 14g | Carbs 35g | Salt 2g |Sugar 17g |Fibers 6g

KETO TUNA SALAD

INGREDIENTS

- 1 CUP OF CANNED TUNA, DRAINED
- 1 TSP. OF DRIED ONION FLAKES
- 3 TBSP. OF "REAL" MAYONNAISE
- SALT AND PEPPER

1 MINUTES   2 SERVINGS

Instructions:

- In a bowl, mix the tuna, mayonnaise, and onion flakes.
- Taste after stirring.
- Season to taste with salt and pepper.

Nutritional Values: Calories 248kcal | Protein 20g | Fat 19g | Carbs 2g | Salt 930mg | Sugar 1g | Fibers 8g

KETO SHRIMP & GRITS

INGREDIENTS

- 3 CUPS OF CAULIFLOWER HEAD
- CAULIFLOWER GRITS
- 2 CUPS OF CHICKEN BROTH
- 1 CUP OF CHEDDAR, SHREDDED
- 2 OZ. CREAM CHEESE
- 1/4 TSP. OF SALT
- 1/4 TSP. OF PEPPER
- 1 TBSP. OF BUTTER
- 3-4 TBSP. OF GREEN ONIONS

CAJUN SHRIMP
- 1/2 TBSP. OF GARLIC, MINCED
- 1 LB. OF PEELED, DEVEINED SHRIMP
- 1/2 TBSP. OF PAPRIKA
- 1/4 TSP. OF ONION POWDER
- 1 TSP. OF ITALIAN SEASONING
- 1/4 TSP. OF GARLIC POWDER
- 2 TBSP. OF BUTTER, DIVIDED
- 1/8 TSP. OF RED PEPPER
- 1/4 TSP. SALT
- 1/4 TSP. OF PEPPER
- 1/4 CUP OF HEAVY CREAM

30 MINUTES   2 SERVINGS

Instructions:

To Make Grits:

- Combine the florets and broth to a medium stock pan and cook over medium heat until cooked.

- When the cauliflower is soft, drain the leftover water and mash the cauliflower with cheddar cheese, cream cheese, butter, pepper, and salt until it resembles grits.

- While you prepare the shrimp, cover the grits to keep them warm.

To make the shrimp, follow these steps:

- Melt 1 tablespoon butter in a large pan over medium heat, then add garlic and shrimp to the skillet, along with the Cajun seasonings. Stir well to ensure that everything is uniformly covered.

- Cook the shrimp for 3-4 minutes, until pink and soft, then whisk in the butter with heavy cream to make the creamy sauce.

- To make the shrimp and grits, split the cauliflower grits among four dishes, then add shrimp and a dribble of cream sauce. Garnish with green onions.

Nutritional Values: *Calories 401kcal | Protein 33g | Fat 28g | Carbs 6g | Salt 1g |Sugar 2g |Fibers 1.6g*

AHI POKE BOWL

INGREDIENTS

- 1 TSP. OF LIME JUICE
- 0.13 CUP OF COCONUT AMINOS
- 1/2 LB. OF SUSHI GRADE TUNA
- 1 TSP. OF SESAME OIL

CAULIFLOWER RICE:
- 1 TBSP. OF AVOCADO OIL
- 6 OZ. OF FRESH CAULIFLOWER RICE
- A PINCH OF BLACK PEPPER
- 1/4 TSP. OF SEA SALT

POKE BOWLS:
- 1/2 CUP OF THINLY SLICED CUCUMBERS
- 1/2 THINLY SLICED AVOCADO
- 1/2 CUP THINLY SLICED RADISHES
- GREEN ONIONS FOR GARNISHING, THINLY SLICED
- SPICY MAYO TO TASTE
- SESAME SEEDS FOR GARNISH, OPTIONAL

5 MINUTES   2 SERVINGS

Instructions:

- Mix together the lime juice, coconut aminos, and sesame oil in a medium mixing bowl. Toss in the tuna to coat it. Cover and chill for up to 2 hours while you prep the remaining ingredients.

- Transfer mayo to a tiny squeeze bottle or use a small zip lock bag with the corner clipped if you don't have one.

- Place the cauliflower rice in four bowls. 1/4 cup cucumbers, 1/4 cup radishes, 1/4 avocado, and 1/2 cup tuna on top of each salad.

- Drizzle the spicy mayo over the bowls in a zig-zag manner. Top with green onions or sesame seeds, if preferred.

Nutritional Values: Calories 450 kcal | Protein 29.6g | Fat 31g | Carbs 7.7g | Salt 560mg |Sugar 2g |Fibers 5.9g

TUNA ZUCCHINI BOATS

INGREDIENTS

- 1/2 LARGE DICED RED BELL PEPPER
- 2 TSP. OF AVOCADO OIL
- 2 CANS OF CHILI LIME WILD TUNA
- 2 ZUCCHINIS, LARGE
- 1/2 CUP OF SALSA
- SALT AND PEPPER
- A PINCH OF CUMIN

FOR THE AVOCADO SALSA:
- 1/4 CUP OF CHOPPED CILANTRO
- 1 SMALL AVOCADO, CUBED
- 2 TSP. OF FRESH LIME JUICE
- 3 TBSP. OF MINCED RED ONION

20 MINUTES   2 SERVINGS

Instructions:

- Preheat the oven to 400°F and coat a baking tray using avocado oil.

- In a medium frying pan, heat the avocado oil over moderate heat. Cook until the chopped pepper is soft. Remove the pan from the heat and toss in the undrained tuna with salsa and stir until fully blended.

- Trim the zucchini's ends, then cut it in half lengthwise and scoop out the interior, creating 1/2-inch shells. Add a sprinkle of salt, pepper, and cumin to taste.

- Distribute the tuna mixture evenly among all of the shells, firmly pushing it in and heaping it high up so that everything fits.

- Bake for 15-20 minutes.

- Mix all of the salsa components in a dish and salt to taste while the zucchini bakes.

- Consume the salsa after it has been served over the boats.

Nutritional Values: Calories 417kcal | Protein 39g | Fat 20.8g | Carbs 24.5g | Salt 868.7mg |Sugar 6.5g |Fibers 9.3g

BAKED SALMON

INGREDIENTS

- 1 2/3 FRESH HERBS OF CHOICE
- 2/3 LB. SALMON BONELESS
- 2/3 TBSP. OF EXTRA VIRGIN OLIVE OIL
- 2/3 SMALL, DIVIDED LEMONS
- 1/3 TSP. OF KOSHER SALT
- 1 GARLIC PEELED AND ROUGHLY CHOPPED
- A PINCH OF GROUNDED BLACK PEPPER

15 MINUTES   2 SERVINGS

Instructions:

- Take the salmon out from the fridge and set it aside for 10 mins to come to room temperature as you make the remaining ingredients. Preheat the oven to 375 degrees Fahrenheit. Using a big piece of aluminum foil, line a rimmed baking sheet.

- Spray the foil with aluminum baking spray, then place two rosemary sprigs down the center. Slice one of the lemons to thin slices and place half of them along with the rosemary down the center. On top of it, place the salmon.

- Drizzle the olive oil over the fish and season with salt and pepper. After rubbing to coat, sprinkle the garlic cloves on top. On top of the salmon, scatter the leftover rosemary and lemon segments. Pour the juice from the second lemon over the top.

- Fold the aluminum foil sides up over the salmon to fully encapsulate it. Place the second sheet of foil atop and tuck the edges under to make a sealed package if your first piece isn't big enough. Allow a little amount of space within the tinfoil for air to flow.

- Bake for 15-20 minutes, or until the thickest portion of the salmon is nearly entirely cooked through.

- Retrieve the fish from the oven and gently unwrap the foil to expose the whole top. Place the salmon in the oven to broil for 5 min, or until the salmon and garlic are slightly brown and the salmon is cooked throughout. Take the fish out of the oven. If it still seems underdone, put the foil over it again and set it aside for a few mins. Allow it to sit for a short time—salmon may easily go from "not done" to "overdone." It's ready when it readily flakes with a fork.
- Cut the fish into chunks to serve. As desired, top with more fresh herbs or a squeeze of lemon.

Nutritional Values: Calories 180kcal | Protein 28g | Fat 6g | Carbs 4g | Salt 789mg |Sugar 2g |Fibers 1g

COCONUT MILK POPSICLES

INGREDIENTS

- ⅙ CUP OF BLUEBERRIES
- ⅓ CAN OF COCONUT MILK
- ⅔ TBSP. OF MINT LEAVES
- ⅙ OZ. OF LIME JUICE

5 MINUTES · **2 SERVINGS**

Instructions:

- In a saucepan, heat the coconut milk with the mint leaves and cook for 4-5 minutes. Remove the pan from the heat. Remove the leaves and let the coconut milk cool.

- To make a sugar-free compote, mix lime juice with blueberries in a skillet over low flame for 4-5 mins. Let the compote cool fully before serving.

- Fill six popsicle molds approximately 34% full with room temperature coconut milk. If using big molds, a tiny quantity of water may be added to each to help with volume. Freeze for 30-40 minutes or until the mixture is somewhat set.

- Remove the fruit compote from the freezer and stir it in. Place popsicle sticks in the middle of the molds and freeze for at least two hours, just until the popsicles are totally frozen.

Nutritional Values: *Calories 133kcal | Protein 1g | Fat 13g | Carbs 3g | Salt 8mg | Sugar 1g | Fibers 0g*

WHITE CHOCOLATE AND PEANUT BUTTER FAT BOMBS

INGREDIENTS

- 3 TBSP. OF PEANUT BUTTER, SUGAR-FREE
- 3 TBSP. OF SOFTENED CREAM CHEESE
- 4 OZ. WHITE CHOCOLATE CHIPS, SUGAR-FREE
- 1 TSP. OF VANILLA EXTRACT
- 1/4 CUP OF COCONUT FLOUR
- 1 TBSP. OF ERYTHRITOL

15 MINUTES   2 SERVINGS

Instructions:

- In a blender, combine all the ingredients except the chocolate chips. Pulse until the mixture is completely smooth.
- Divide the dough into spheres and roll them out.
- Set aside for approximately an hour to chill.
- Microwave the white chips for 30 seconds at a time.
- Dip each fat bomb into the ganache until completely covered.
- Refrigerate until ready

Nutritional Values: Calories 41 kcal | Protein 1.5g | Fat 4g | Carbs 3g | Salt 100mg |Sugar 52g |Fibers 0.8 g

CHOCOLATE MUG CAKE

INGREDIENTS

- 1 TBSP. OF COCOA POWDER
- 2 TBSP. OF ALMOND FLOUR
- 1 TSP. OF WATER
- 1 TBSP. OF LOW CARB SUGAR
- 1 TBSP. OF MAYONNAISE
- 1/4 TSP. OF BAKING POWDER
- 1 EGG YOLK

1 MINUTES   2 SERVINGS

Instructions:

- Fill a cup or jelly jar halfway with dry ingredients and stir well with a fork.

- Stir in the egg yolk, mayonnaise, and water until well combined, being careful to scrape the bottom of the pan. Allow 1-2 minutes for the batter to rest.

- Depending on your microwave, microwave for 50 seconds.

Nutritional Values: Calories 272kcal | Protein 9g | Fat 23g | Carbs 7g | Salt 30mg |Sugar 1g |Fibers4g

CHOCO-ORANGE BALLS

INGREDIENTS

- 2 CUPS OF MACADAMIA NUTS
- 1 TBSP. OF CHIA SEEDS
- 1 1/3 CUPS OF DESICCATED COCONUT
- 2 TBSP. OF CACAO POWDER
- 2 TBSP. OF XYLITOL
- 1 TBSP. OF ORANGE ZEST
- PINCH OF SEA SALT
- 1/2 TBSP. OF MELTED BUTTER, COOLED

1 MINUTES 2 SERVINGS

Instructions:

- In a dish, combine the chia seed with 2 tablespoons of water. Allow it to sit for 10 minutes, stirring regularly, until the water has been soaked and the mixture has taken on a gel-like consistency.

- In a food processor, combine the macadamias, xylitol, cacao powder, 1 cup coconut, zest, chia mixture, butter, and salt. Process until the ingredients are finely minced and well blended.

- Place the nut mixture in a mixing dish. Make balls out of level tablespoonful of the ingredients. Place the rest of the coconut on a platter. To gently cover the balls with coconut, roll them in it.

- Refrigerate for up to 1 week in an airtight container.

Nutritional Values: Calories 165kcal | Protein 2g | Fat 16.5g | Carbs 1g | Salt 25mg | Sugar 900mg | Fibers 2.5g

CHOCO-COFFEE CANDY

INGREDIENTS

- 2 OZ. OF RAW CACAO BUTTER
- 1 1/2 TBSP. OF STRING GROUND COFFEE
- 6 OZ. SUGAR-FREE MILK CHOCOLATE
- 8 OZ. SUGAR-FREE DARK CHOCOLATE

1 MINUTES   2 SERVINGS

Instructions:

1. Preheat the oven to 350°F. Prep a baking sheet using parchment paper and place it in the refrigerator.

2. Combine the cacao butter with dark chocolate in a large bowl. Microwave on high for 30 seconds, stirring after each, fully melted.

3. Toss the milk chocolate into the mixing bowl. Microwave on high for 20 seconds, stirring after each until chocolate is fully melted. Allow resting until the cacao butter has completely melted.

4. Add the ground coffee and stir to combine. With a spoon, spread the mixture evenly on the parchment paper.

5. Refrigerate the baking sheet till the chocolate is totally set and cool. Cut the chocolate into small pieces. Serve and have fun!

Nutritional Values: *Calories 348kcal | Protein 26g | Fat 6g | Carbs 56g | Salt 1578mg | Sugar 15g | Fibers 18g*

KETO PEANUT BUTTER

INGREDIENTS

- 2 CUPS OF DRY ROASTED PEANUTS
- SEA SALT
- ERYTHRITOL OR STEVIA OPTIONAL

5 MINUTES   **2 SERVINGS**

Instructions:

- In a food processor, blend peanuts for 4 mins. Run for a shorter time if you want chunky peanut butter. Run for a longer time if you want smoother peanut butter.

- Season with salt to taste.

- The use of a sweetener is completely optional. Stir in stevia if you want sweeter peanut butter.

Nutritional Values: *Calories 71kcal | Protein 3g | Fat 6g | Carbs 3g | Salt 6mg |Sugar 0.6g |Fibers 1g*

KETO SNACK BARS

INGREDIENTS

- 1/2 CUP OF MACADAMIA NUTS
- 1 CUP OF DESICCATED COCONUT
- 1/2 CUP OF WALNUT HALVES
- 1 TSP. OF GROUND CINNAMON
- 1/2 CUP OF PEPITAS
- 1/2 CUP OF PEANUT COCONUT SPREAD
- 1/4 CUP OF COCONUT OIL SOLIDIFIED
- 2 TSP. OF VANILLA BEAN PASTE
- 1/2 CUP OF ALMONDS

180 MINUTES 2 SERVINGS

Instructions:

- Using the baking paper, lightly oil and line a lamington pan. In a food processor, finely chop the walnuts, macadamia nuts, almonds, and pepitas. Place in a large mixing bowl. Combine the coconut & cinnamon with the nut mix in a mixing bowl.

- In a small saucepan, mix the peanut paste, coconut oil, and vanilla and simmer, constantly stirring, over low flame for 3-5 min, or until dissolved and thoroughly blended.

- Mix the peanut butter mixture into the dry ingredients until everything is completely blended. Smooth the top with the spoon after pressing the mixture firmly into the prepared pan. Cover and chill for at least 2 hours, or until hard. Cut the cake into 16 bars.

Nutritional Values: *Calories 237kcal | Protein 6g | Fat 22g | Carbs 3g | Salt 41mg | Sugar | Fibers 3g*

ROSEMARY SPICED NUTS

INGREDIENTS

- 1 LB. RAW MIX NUTS
- 1 TBSP. OF AVOCADO OIL
- 3/4 TSP. OF SALT
- 1/2 TSP. OF DRIED SAGE
- 1 TBSP. OF FRESH ROSEMARY

20 MINUTES   2 SERVINGS

Instructions:

- Preheat your oven to 300 degrees Fahrenheit.

- Finely dice fresh rosemary

- Mix the avocado oil, salt, dry powdered sage, and rosemary in a large mixing bowl.

- Toss in the mixed nuts and toss well until evenly covered.

- On the sheet pan, place parchment paper or a silicone liner. In the same pan, add the mixed nuts.

- Preheat oven to 300°F and bake for 10 minutes. Remove the nuts after 10 minutes and stir well.

- Return the nuts to the oven for ten min after stirring.

- Remove the nuts from the oven after 20 minutes and let them cool fully before eating.

Nutritional Values: *Calories 352kcal | Protein 9g | Fat 30g | Carbs 14g | Salt 1g |Sugar 500mg |Fibers 5g*

SEED BREAD LOAF

INGREDIENTS

- 1/2 CUP OF PSYLLIUM HUSKS
- 1 CUP OF SUNFLOWER SEEDS
- 1/2 CUP OF FLAX SEEDS
- 1 1/2 CUPS OF RAW PUMPKIN SEEDS
- 1 TSP. OF FINE SEA SALT
- A PINCH OF POWDERED STEVIA
- 3 TBSP. OF OLIVE OIL
- 1/2 CUP OF CHIA SEEDS
- 1 1/2 CUPS OF WARM WATER

60 MINUTES   2 SERVINGS

Instructions:

- Heat the oven at 350 degrees and put aside a 1 lb. loaf pan lined with parchment paper.

- In a blender, process 1 cup of pumpkin seeds until fine minced. It should have the consistency of medium-coarse flour.

- Mix the pumpkin seed flour with the remaining pumpkin seeds, sunflower seeds, psyllium husks, flax seeds, salt, chia seeds, and maple syrup in a mixing bowl.

- After that, mix in water & olive oil until a batter forms.

- Bake approximately 45 minutes, pressing the mixture into the pan with your hands.

- Remove the bread from the loaf pan and set it aside. Return the loaf to the oven and bake for fifteen minutes with the top down on the sheet pan.

- When you tap the bread, and it feels hollow within, it's done.

- Allow it to cool fully before slicing into 16 pieces.

- Toast the bread before serving.

Nutritional Values: Calories 160 kcal | Protein 7g | Fat 14g | Carbs 2g | Salt 86mg | Sugar 0.2g | Fibers 8g

BROCCOLI TOTS

INGREDIENTS

- 1/2 LB. BROCCOLI
- 1/8 CUP OF GROUND FLAX
- 1/4 CUP OF ALMOND FLOUR
- 1/2 TSP. OF SALT
- 1/4 TSP. OF GARLIC POWDER

25 MINUTES   2 SERVINGS

Instructions:

- Broccoli should be chopped.

- Steam the chopped broccoli for 4 minutes.

- Using a food processor, pulverize the broccoli until it resembles rice.

- Combine the riced broccoli, almond flour, salt, ground flax, and garlic powder in a large mixing bowl.

- Combine the broccoli and the other ingredients in a mixing bowl and set aside for a few minutes to meld together.

- By pushing the mix into your palm and making tots with the thumb and pointer of the other hand, make 18-20 broccoli tots. Firmly press the ingredients together.

- Bake for 20 minutes at 375 degrees F, turning after 5 minutes to brown both sides.

Nutritional Values: Calories 172 kcal | Protein 8g | Fat 12g | Carbs 14g | Salt 940mg |Sugar 3g |Fibers 7g

ZUCCHINI NOODLES

INGREDIENTS

- 2 MEDIUM ZUCCHINIS
- 2 TBSP. OF BUTTER
- 3 CLOVES OF MINCED GARLIC
- 3/4 CUP OF PARMESAN CHEESE
- KOSHER SALT AND PEPPER
- 1/4 TSP. OF CHILI FLAKES

10 MINUTES   2 SERVINGS

Instructions:

- Using a julienne peeler, trim zucchini to spirals. Remove the noodles and set them aside.

- Preheat a large skillet over medium-high heat. After the butter has melted, add the garlic. Cook for 30 seconds, or until garlic is aromatic and transparent. Make sure the garlic doesn't burn.

- Cook until zucchini noodles are soft, approximately 3-5 minutes. Zucchini noodles cook quickly, so taste a strand while they're cooking.

- Remove the skillet from the heat, sprinkle with parmesan cheese, and season to taste with pepper and salt. Serve heated with chili flakes.

Nutritional Values: Calories 283kcal | Protein 16g | Fat 21g | Carbs 7g | Salt 720mg |Sugar 5g |Fibers 1g

VEGETABLE SOUP

INGREDIENTS

- 2 TBSP. OF OLIVE OIL
- 1 LARGE, DICED ONION
- 2 LARGE, DICED BELL PEPPERS
- 4 MINCED CLOVES OF GARLIC
- 1 MEDIUM HEAD OF CAULIFLOWER, FLORIATED
- 2 CUPS OF TRIMMED GREEN BEANS, CHOPPED TO 1 INCH
- 2 14.5-OZ. CANS OF DICED TOMATOES
- 8 CUPS OF CHICKEN/VEGETABLE BROTH
- 1 TBSP. OF ITALIAN SEASONING
- 2 BAY LEAVES, DRIED
- SEA SALT AND PEPPER

30 MINUTES   2 SERVINGS

Instructions:

- In a pot, heat the olive oil over moderate flame.
- Toss in the bell peppers and onions. Cook, occasionally stirring, for 7 to 10 minutes, or until onions are transparent and browned.
- Add the garlic, minced. Cook, occasionally stirring, for approximately a minute or until aromatic.
- Cauliflower, diced tomatoes, stock, green beans, and Italian spice are added to the pan. Toss in a pinch of sea salt and a pinch of pepper to taste. If using, add the bay leaves.
- Toss the soup in a pot with enough water to cover it and bring to a boil. Cook for 15 minutes, covered, over medium-low heat, until vegetables are tender.

Nutritional Values: Calories 79kcal | Protein 2g | Fat 2g | Carbs 11g | Salt 1344mg |Sugar 800mg |Fibers 3g

CAULIFLOWER MAC & CHEESE

INGREDIENTS

- 1/2 FLORIATED HEAD OF CAULIFLOWER
- 1 1/2 TBSP. OF BUTTER
- SEA SALT AND PEPPER
- 1/2 CUP OF SHREDDED CHEDDAR CHEESE
- 1/9 CUP OF HEAVY CREAM
- 1/9 CUP ALMOND MILK, UNSWEETENED

20 MINUTES 2 SERVINGS

Instructions:

- Heat your oven to 450°F. Use foil to line a baking sheet.

- 2 tablespoons of butter should be melted. Toss the florets with the butter melt in a large mixing dish. Season with salt and pepper.

- Spread the florets on the baking sheet that has been prepared. Roast until crisp-tender, approximately 10-15 minutes.

- Warm the heavy cream, milk, cheddar cheese, and leftover butter, stirring constantly. Heat the cheese mixture until it is completely smooth. Be cautious not to burn the cheese by overheating it.

- Just before serving, toss the cauliflower with the cheese sauce.

Nutritional Values: *Calories 294kcal | Protein 11g | Fat 23g | Carbs 12g | Salt 20mg |Sugar 30mg |Fibers 5g*

BLUEBERRY PLEASURE SMOOTHIE

INGREDIENTS

- 1/2 CUP UNSWEETENED ALMOND MILK
- 1/2 CUP OF MIXED BERRIES OR FROZEN BLUEBERRIES
- 2 SCOOPS OF HEMEPROTEIN POWDER
- 1/2 CUP OF STEAMED CAULIFLOWER, THEN FREEZE
- 1/4 TSP CINNAMON
- 1 TBSP HONEY
- 1/2 CUP WATER

5 MINUTES   2 SERVINGS

Instructions:

- Steam the cauliflower until it is soft (about 5 to 7 min)

- Set cauliflower on a baking sheet and place in the freezer for at minimum 2 hours.

- Blend all of the ingredients in a blender at high speed until smooth

Nutritional Values: *Calories 94kcals | Protein 7g | Fat | Carbs 15g | Salt 65mg |Sugar 2g |Fibers 2g*

CHEESE & SPINACH PIE

INGREDIENTS

- 4.4 OZ. OF SPINACH
- 2 1/2 EGGS
- 3/4 CUP OF CHEDDAR CHEESE
- 1 TOMATO
- 1/4 TSP. OF GARLIC POWDER
- 1/2 TSP. OF NUTMEG
- 1/2 TSP. OF ONION POWDER
- 1/2 TBSP. OF BASIL
- 1/2 TBSP. OF OREGANO
- SALT AND PEPPER
- 1/2 TBSP. OLIVE OIL

35 MINUTES 2 SERVINGS

Instructions:

- Heat your oven to 200 degrees Celsius.
- In a large mixing basin, whisk together the eggs.
- Combine the garlic, onion powder, nutmeg, salt, and pepper in a mixing bowl.
- Cheese should be grated.
- Stir everything together, then add the spinach & cheese.
- Ensure that everything is well-coated in the egg and spice mixture.
- Pour into a 9-inch pie pan that has been greased with a little oil, spread evenly, and bake!
- Tomatoes should be sliced.
- Remove the pie after 20 - 30 min of cooking and arrange the tomato on top.
- Cook for a further 15-20 minutes.
- When the pasta is done, add the basil, oregano, and a pinch of salt and pepper.

Nutritional Values: Calories 315kcal | Protein 20g | Fat 23g | Carbs 7g | Salt 395mg | Sugar 3g | Fibers 3g

BROCCOLI SALAD

INGREDIENTS

- 1 1/2 CUPS OF BROCCOLI FLORETS
- 1/4 CUP OF DICED RED ONION
- 1 1/2 BACON STRIPS
- 1/9 CUP OF DRIED CRANBERRIES
- 1/9 CUP OF SHREDDED WHITE CHEDDAR CHEESE
- 3/4 TBSP. SUNFLOWER SEEDS, ROASTED
- ·HONEY MUSTARD DRESSING
- 3/4 TBSP. OF DIJON MUSTARD
- A DRIZZLE OF HONEY
- 3/4 TBSP. OLIVE OIL
- 1/2 TBSP. APPLE CIDER VINEGAR
- 1/9 TSP. OF GARLIC POWDER
- SALT AND PEPPER

15 MINUTES   2 SERVINGS

Instructions:

- In a large mixing basin, combine all the salad ingredients.

- In a blender, combine all dressing ingredients and blend until smooth. Add water as needed to get the desired consistency. Taste, then season with salt and pepper, if necessary, before pouring over the broccoli salad.

- Toss the salad in the dressing to coat it. Serve right away or refrigerate for 24 hours.

Nutritional Values: Calories 200 kcal | Protein 6 g | Fat 12 g | Carbs 21 g, | Salt 227 mg |Sugar 15 g |Fibers 3 g

DEVILED EGGS (MAYO-LESS)

INGREDIENTS

- 2 EGGS, LARGE
- 1/3 RIPE AVOCADO
- 2/3 TBSP. EXTRA VIRGIN OLIVE OIL
- 1/3 TSP. OF WHITE WINE VINEGAR
- 1/3 TSP. CAPERS
- PINCH OF DIJON MUSTARD
- 1/3 TBSP. MINCED JALAPENO
- 1/3 MINCED CLOVE OF GARLIC
- 1/3 TBSP. CILANTRO
- A PINCH PAPRIKA
- SALT AND PEPPER
- 1/3 THINLY SLICED RADISH
- 1/3 TBSP. OF CHOPPED CHIVES

15 MINUTES 2 SERVINGS

Instructions:

- In the bottom of a pot, arrange eggs in a layer. 2 inches of water should be used to cover them. Bring the water to a boil. Turn off the heat, cover it, and set it aside for 10-12 minutes. While you wait, fill a big dish halfway with cold water. With a slotted spoon, remove your eggs and set them in the cool water. This will bring the cooking to a halt. Allow for a minute of cooling before peeling.
- Remove the yolks from each egg by slicing it in half lengthwise. Put them in the food processor's bowl. Combine the avocado, vinegar, capers, mustard, olive oil, jalapeño, cilantro, paprika, salt, olive oil, and pepper in the food processor bowl. Pulse for 4-5 seconds at a time at 1-second intervals. Salt to taste and add more if required.
- Fill a piping bag with the yolk mixture and the star tip. Fill each egg white hole with the mixture.
- Serve eggs with a radish slice and chives as a garnish.

Nutritional Values: Calories 80kcal | Protein 3g | Fat 7g | Carbs 2g | Salt 87mg | Sugar 1g | Fibers 1g

EGG SALAD

INGREDIENTS

- 3 EGGS
- 2 TBSP FINELY DICED RED ONION
- SALT AND PEPPER
- 1/2 TBSP. OF DIJON MUSTARD
- 1 TBSP. OF DICED PARSLEY
- 2 TBSP OF MAYONNAISE
- 1 TBSP. OF DICED CHIVES
- 1/2 TSP. OF LEMON JUICE

15 MINUTES   2 SERVINGS

Instructions:

- A kettle of water should be brought to a boil. Then reduce the heat to a low setting to avoid any bubbles. Put the eggs in the saucepan slowly and carefully using a skimmer. Return the heat to high and continue to cook the eggs for another 12 minutes.

- To halt the cooking process and chill the eggs, place them in cold water.

- When your eggs are cold enough to handle, peel them and throw the shells. Cut the hard-cooked eggs to the size you want. Then, in a mixing dish, combine the eggs, chives, Dijon mustard, parsley, mayonnaise, red onion, and lemon juice.

- Serve in a dish, in a bagel, or in a tortilla with pepper and salt.

Nutritional Values: Calories 197kcal | Protein 8g | Fat 16g | Carbs 1g | Salt 226mg |Sugar 1g |Fibers 1g

CAULIFLOWER "BREADSTICKS"

INGREDIENTS

- 1/2 FLORIATED HEAD OF CAULIFLOWER
- 1 CLOVES OF GARLIC
- 1/4 CUP OF MOZZARELLA CHEESE, SHREDDED
- 1/4 CUP PARMESAN CHEESE, GRATED
- 1 LIGHTLY BEATEN EGGS
- 1 EGG WHITE
- 1/2 TBSP. FRESH THYME, CHOPPED
- 1/2 TBSP. FRESH ROSEMARY, CHOPPED
- KOSHER SALT AND PEPPER
- 1 TBSP. EXTRA-VIRGIN OLIVE OIL

20 MINUTES 2 SERVINGS

Instructions:

- Heat your oven to 425 degrees Fahrenheit. Using parchment paper, line a baking sheet.

- Mix the cauliflower florets with garlic in a food processor. Pulse for 3 minutes or until the mix becomes a fine meal. In a mixing dish, combine all of the ingredients.

- Toss the cauliflower with the thyme, mozzarella, eggs, egg white, parmesan, and rosemary until well incorporated; add salt and pepper.

- On the baking sheet, form the cauliflower mix into a 12-inch-thick circle. Apply the olive oil over the whole surface. Bake for 25 to 30 minutes, or until crisp.

- Allow it cool for 5 mins before cutting and serving.

Nutritional Values: Calories 200kcal | Protein 12g | Fat 14g | Carbs 9g | Salt 780mg | Sugar 3g | Fibers 2g

LOADED CAULIFLOWER

INGREDIENTS

- 1 LB. FLORIATED CAULIFLOWER
- 1/2 CUP OF SOUR CREAM
- 1 CUP OF CHEDDAR CHEESE, GRATED
- 1/2 CUP OF MAYONNAISE
- 4 COOKED BACON SLICES
- 6 TBSP. FRESH CHIVES, CHOPPED
- 3 TBSP. BUTTER
- 1/4 TSP. OF GARLIC POWDER
- SALT AND PEPPER

10 MINUTES 2 SERVINGS

Instructions:

- Firstly, chop the cauliflower florets into tiny pieces.

- Place them all in a mixing dish and bring to a boil. Cover with plastic wrap after adding 2 teaspoons of water. Cook for 5-8 minutes in the oven over medium heat, checking after 8 minutes to ensure they are not overdone.

- Drain the extra water when they've been thoroughly cooked. Wait a moment or two with the lid off. This may be used in the microwave, on the stovetop, or in the oven

- Blend the cauliflower in a food processor, blender, or mixer until it's light and fluffy. Process the garlic powder, butter, and sour cream together until the mixture resembles mashed potatoes.

- Add the chopped fresh chives to the mashed cauliflower in a bowl. Mix in the cheddar cheese by hand or in a blender until well combined. I prefer to add a little mayonnaise, but if you don't like it, leave it out. Finally, season with salt and pepper to suit. All of these elements work nicely together.

- I add chives and bacon for decoration, and the leftover cheese goes on top of the cauliflower dish.

Nutritional Values: Calories 298kcal | Protein 11.6g | Fat 24.6g | Carbs 7.4g | Salt 285mg |Sugar 3.85g |Fibers 3g

CREAMY CHICKEN GARLIC SOUP

INGREDIENTS

- 1 TBSP. BUTTER
- 1 CUP OF SHREDDED CHICKEN
- 2 OZ. CUBED CREAM CHEESE
- 1/8 CUP OF HEAVY CREAM
- 1 TBSP. OF GARLIC GUSTO SEASONING BY STACEY HAWKINS
- 7 1/4 OZ. OF CHICKEN BROTH
- SALT

10 MINUTES   2 SERVINGS

Instructions:

- In a medium saucepan, melt the butter.
- Using melted butter, coat the shredded chicken in the pan.
- Add cream cheese cubes and Garlic Gusto spice as the chicken starts to warm. To combine the components, mix them together
- Add chicken broth as well as heavy cream after the cubes have melted and uniformly distributed. Bring to a simmer, then lower to low heat and continue to cook for 3–4 minutes.
- Serve with a pinch of salt to taste.

Nutritional Values: Calories 307kcal | Protein 18g |Fat 25g | Carbs 2g | Salt 718mg |Sugar 0g |Fibers 0g

CREAM OF CAULIFLOWER

INGREDIENTS

- 1 LARGE FINELY CHOPPED BROWN ONION
- 1 TBSP. OF OLIVE OIL
- 3 TSP. OF CUMIN SEEDS
- 1 LARGE FLORIATED CAULIFLOWER (1.5 KG)
- 1/2 CUP OF POURING CREAM
- 4 CUPS CHICKEN/ VEGETABLE STOCK
- CHOPPED CHIVES

35 MINUTES   2 SERVINGS

Instructions:

- Heat the oil.

- Over medium heat in a big saucepan, Toss in the onion. Reduce the heat to a medium-low setting. Cook, uncovered, for 10 minutes, stirring occasionally. Add the cumin seeds and mix well. Cook for 1 minute, stirring constantly.

- In the same pan, add the cauliflower and the stock. Bring to a boil, covered. Reduce the heat to a low setting. Cook for 20 minutes, slightly covered, or till cauliflower is very soft. Remove the pan from the heat. Allow 10 minutes for cooling.

- In stages, puree the soup until smooth. Return the soup to the pan over a low heat setting. Add the cream and mix well. Cook, occasionally stirring, for 4 mins, or until well heated. Season with salt and pepper.

- The soup should be ladled into bowls. Serve with a dollop of sour cream on top. Garnish with cracked black pepper & chives on top. Serve.

Nutritional Values: Calories 155kcal | Protein 5g| Fat 12g | Carbs 6g | Salt 736mg |Sugar 5g |Fibers4g

CREAMY ASPARAGUS SOUP

INGREDIENTS

- 1 LB. ASPARAGUS
- 1 TBSP. OF UNSALTED BUTTER
- 1/2 CHOPPED YELLOW ONION, MEDIUM
- 1 SMASHED GARLIC CLOVE
- 1/4 CUP OF HEAVY CREAM
- 2 CUPS OF LOW-SODIUM VEGETABLE/CHICKEN BROTH
- 1/2 TBSP. OF LEMON JUICE
- 1/4 CUP OF SHREDDED PARMESAN
- FRESH HERBS
- SALT AND PEPPER

15 MINUTES   2 SERVINGS

Instructions:

- Melt the butter in a big saucepan over medium heat.
- Cook for 6-8 minutes, or until the onion and garlic are transparent and soft. To avoid browning, keep stirring regularly. If necessary, lower the heat.
- Set aside the ends of a couple of asparagus spears that have been cut off.
- Add the remaining spears to the saucepan, chop into 1-inch pieces.
- Combine the broth, pepper, and salt in a mixing bowl.
- Remove the saucepan from the heat after 10 minutes of simmering. Allow for some cooling time.
- Using a regular blender, puree the soup until perfectly smooth.
- Combine the parmesan, heavy cream, and lemon juice in a mixing bowl.
- Garnish with your chosen herbs and a dollop of heavy cream and serve!

Nutritional Values: Calories 240kcal | Protein 8g | Fat 20g | Carbs 9g | Salt 351mg |Sugar 4g |Fibers 3g

KETO CHEESEBURGER SOUP

INGREDIENTS

- 1/4 POUND OF GROUNDED BEEF
- 1/5 CUP GRATED ONION
- 1/5 CUP GRATED CARROTS
- 1/5 CUP GRATED CELERY
- 1/4 TSP. SEA SALT
- 1/5 CUP GRATED CAULIFLOWER
- 3/4 CUPS OF ORGANIC CHICKEN BROTH
- 1/4 TBSP. TOMATO PASTE
- 1/4 CUP SOFTENED CREAM CHEESE
- 1/2 CUPS SHREDDED CHEDDAR CHEESE
- 3/8 CUPS OF HEAVY CREAM
- 1/4 TSP. CREOLE SEASONING
- 1/8 TSP. PEPPER

20 MINUTES   2 SERVINGS

Instructions:

- Brown the ground beef in a large pan or stockpot until pieces form, approximately 5 minutes. Remove any excess grease.

- Cook and add onions, carrots, celery, and cauliflower are softened. Stir in the cheeses until they are completely melted.

- Bring to a boil with the tomato paste, cream, chicken broth, and spices. Reduce heat to low and cook for 5 minutes.

- Serve topped with shredded cheese as well as a dash of creole spice.

Nutritional Values: Calories 412kcal | Protein 21g | Fat 32g | Carbs 8g | Salt 871mg |Sugar 5g |Fibers 1g

CREAM OF MUSHROOMS SOUP

INGREDIENTS

- 1 TBSP UNSALTED BUTTER
- 1/4 TBSP. OF OLIVE OIL
- 2 1/2 CUPS SLICED FRESH BROWN MUSHROOMS
- 1/4 CUP OF HEAVY CREAM
- 1 TSP. OF FRESH THYME
- 1 CUP OF CHICKEN/VEGETABLE BROTH
- 1/4 DICED YELLOW ONION
- 1 MINCED CLOVE OF GARLIC
- 0.13 TSP. OF XANTHAN GUM, IT IS OPTIONAL
- 1/9 CUP OF WHITE WINE
- 1/4 TSP. OF SEA SALT
- SALT, PAPRIKA
- FRESH PARSLEY FOR SERVING

20 MINUTES   2 SERVINGS

Instructions:

1. Melt the butter and oil in a pan over medium-high heat. 2 to 3 minutes in heated butter, until onion is softened. Fry for approximately 1 minute or until the garlic is aromatic.

2. Simmer for 5-7 minutes with the cut mushrooms, 2 tablespoons thyme, and the wine.

3. To make a thicker soup, sprinkle the mushrooms with xanthan gum, mix well, and heat for approximately 2 minutes. Bring the broth to a boil in a separate pot.

4. Reduce the heat to low, cover, and cook for 12-15 minutes, or until the sauce has thickened.

5. Take the soup off the heat and add the heavy cream. Using a stick blender, purée the soup at this step.

6. Taste and season with salt and pepper as desired.

7. Add fresh parsley with thyme to the mix. Serve with toasted and buttered low carb bread.

Nutritional Values: Calories 209kcal | Protein 3g | Fat 19g | Carbs 7g | Salt 1346mg |Sugar 2g |Fibers 1g

BERRIES & CREAM SHAKE

INGREDIENTS

- 1 CUP OF COCONUT MILK
- 1 SCOOP OF COLLAGEN
- 1/3 CUP RASPBERRIES, FROZEN
- 1 TBSP. OF COCONUT OIL
- SWEETENER

5 MINUTES   2 SERVINGS

Instructions:

- Blend all the ingredients until smooth. Serve!

Nutritional Values: Calories 549kcal | Protein 10g | Fat 50g | Carbs 10g | Salt 10mg |Sugar 6g |Fibers 3g

STRAWBERRY CHIA ZUCCHINI SMOOTHIE

INGREDIENTS

- 1 CUP OF WATER
- 1/2 CUP STRAWBERRIES, FROZEN
- 1 CUP ZUCCHINI, CHOPPED
- 3 TBSP. CHIA SEEDS

5 MINUTES   2 SERVINGS

Instructions:

- Blend all the ingredients until smooth. Serve!

Nutritional Values: Calories 549kcal | Protein 10g | Fat 50g | Carbs 10g | Salt 10mg |Sugar 6g |Fibers 3g

PEANUT BUTTER SMOOTHIE

INGREDIENTS

- 1 CUP ALMOND MILK, UNSWEETENED
- 2 TBSP. OF NATURAL PEANUT BUTTER, SUGAR FREE
- 3 TBSP. XYLITOL
- 1/4 CUP OF HEAVY CREAM
- 1 CUP OF ICE, CRUSHED
- 1 TBSP. COCOA POWDER, UNSWEETENED

5 MINUTES   2 SERVINGS

Instructions:

- Blend all the ingredients until smooth. Serve!

Nutritional Values: Calories 172kcal | Protein 5.2g | Fat 15.4g | Carbs 4.7g | Salt 8mg |Sugar 2.2g |Fibers 3g

AVOCADO MINT SMOOTHIE

INGREDIENTS

- 3-4 OZ. AVOCADO
- 1 1/2 CUP OF COCONUT MILK, FULL FAT
- 1 CUP OF ALMOND MILK
- SUGAR SUBSTITUTE
- 10 MINT LEAVES. LARGE
- 6 CILANTRO SPRIGS
- 2 SQUEEZES OF LIME JUICE
- 1/2 TSP. VANILLA
- 2 CUPS OF CRUSHED ICE

5 MINUTES   2 SERVINGS

Instructions:

- Blend all the ingredients until smooth. Serve!

Nutritional Values: Calories 223kcal | Protein 1g | Fat 23g | Carbs 5g | Salt 110mg | Sugar 3g | Fibers 1g

DOUBLE CHOCOLATE SMOOTHIE

INGREDIENTS

- 1/2 AVOCADO
- 1 TBSP. OF CACAO POWDER
- 3/4 CUP OF ALMOND MILK
- 1 SERVING OF CHOCOLATE PROTEIN POWDER, KETO-FRIENDLY
- 1 TBSP. OF CHIA SEEDS
- 1/4 CUP OF COCONUT MILK, FULL FAT

5 MINUTES   2 SERVINGS

Instructions:

- Blend all the ingredients until smooth. Serve!

Nutritional Values: Calories 223kcal | Protein 1g | Fat 23g | Carbs 5g | Salt 110mg |Sugar 3g |Fibers 1g

4 WEEK MEAL PLAN

WEEK	BREAKFAST	LUNCH	SNACK	DINNER
1 WEEK	*Peanut butter smoothie*	*Greek Chicken*	*Keto Snack Bars*	*Cream of Cauliflower*
2 WEEK	*Green Eggs*	*Easy Lattuce Wrap*	*Broccoli Tots*	*Loaded Cauliflower*
3 WEEK	*Keto Mug Bread*	*Keto Pizza*	*Keto Peanut Butter*	*Keto Cheeseburger Soup*
4 WEEK	*Simple Breakfast Sandwich*	*Stuffed Sausages*	*Strawberry Chia Zucchini Smoothie*	*Broccoli salad*

KETO DIET PLAN

Week 1	Breakfast	Lunch	Dinner
Monday			
Tuesday			
Wednesday			
Thursday			
Friday			
Saturday			
Sunday			

Conclusion

There is no such thing as a "standard" keto with a set macronutrient ratio. The keto diet puts a limit on total carbohydrate consumption to less than 50 g each day, which is even less than a standard plain bagel, and maybe as little as 20 g per day. Popular ketogenic sites recommend total daily calories of 70-80 percent fat, 5-10 percent carbohydrate, and 10-20 percent protein. This equates to around 165 g of fat, 40 g of carbohydrate, and 75 g of protein in a 2000-calorie diet. Because consuming too much protein might hinder ketosis, the protein consumption on the ketogenic diet is maintained modest compared to other low-carb, high-protein diets. Because protein's amino acids may be transformed to glucose, a ketogenic diet must include enough protein to maintain lean body mass, including muscle, while still causing ketosis.

There are many different types of ketogenic diets, but they all exclude carbohydrate-rich meals. Starch granules from both processed and whole grains, such as pieces of bread, pasta, rice, cereals, and cookies; potatoes, maize, and other starchy foods; and fruit juices, to name a few. Legumes, beans, and most fruits are among the less apparent. Most ketogenic diets include saturated fat-rich foods like fat pieces of meat, deli meats, lard, and butter, and also unsaturated fat-rich foods like nuts, avocados, plant oils, seeds, and oily fish. Ketogenic meal lists might differ and even clash depending on where you get your data.

If you want to lose weight, bear in mind that the plan will most likely entail a full change in your eating habits. However, if you're trying to lose weight or maybe have some of the health issues it's been proved to aid with, it will be worth it. The ketogenic is one of the healthiest and trendiest diets available and will surely benefit the people who look to follow it.

Manufactured by Amazon.ca
Bolton, ON